Original Title: Wanderlust Whispers

Copyright © 2024 Book Fairy Publishing
All rights reserved.

Editors: Theodor Taimla
Autor: Paul Pääsuke
ISBN 978-9916-748-02-2

Wanderlust Whispers

Paul Pääsuke

Following the River of Stars

Beneath the velvet sky, we set our sights,
Guided by the river of stars, so bright.
Its flow charts our course through the tranquil nights,
On a journey beyond the edge of light.

In its waters, mirrored dreams and thoughts,
Galaxies swirling in the depths unseen.
Each star a story, its brilliance caught,
In the flow, we find places we've never been.

With each stroke, we sail through cosmic seas,
Following the current wherever it leads.
Past constellations and mysteries,
On this river, the soul of adventure feeds.

For in the sky, there lies paths untold,
Within the stars, our destiny unfolds.

Odyssey of the Untamed Heart

An untamed heart sets forth on an odyssey,
Beyond the reaches of the mundane and known.
Seeking out where the wild spirits roam free,
In places where seeds of dreams are sown.

Through forests deep, where ancient whispers call,
Over mountains high, touching skies untold.
The heart, a traveler, climbs after each fall,
Its courage and fervor ever bold.

Across vast deserts, under the scorching sun,
It journeys, driven by a quest for more.
Through hardships faced, and battles won,
The heart grows stronger than ever before.

Untamed and free, it finds its way at last,
In the odyssey of journeys vast.

In the Embrace of Unfamiliar Winds

In the embrace of unfamiliar winds,
We find our sails unfurled and spirits high.
Emboldened by the change that it brings,
We chart a course under the open sky.

With each gust, a new path unfolds,
Carrying us to lands unknown.
The unknown breeze, a story it holds,
Whispering secrets in a tone, all its own.

Through storms and calms, the winds guide,
Pushing us beyond our fear and doubt.
In their embrace, we learn to glide,
Discovering what life is truly about.

So let the unfamiliar winds blow,
For in their call, we truly grow.

The Call of the Untrodden Path

There's a call that whispers in the silent woods,
A call from the untrodden path, so clear.
It beckons to those whose hearts seek the goods,
Of adventures born from the frontier.

With every step, the path winds and twists,
Through ancient woods and over brooks serene.
By fog and moonlight, the trail is kissed,
Revealing wonders so rarely seen.

This path, it teaches us to trust,
In the journey and in our own stride.
With every footprint, we adjust,
Embracing each moment, wide-eyed.

So follow the call, let your heart lead,
On the untrodden path, your soul will feed.

The Soul's Endless Pilgrimage

Upon life's vast, unfolding scroll,
In search of solace, depth, and role,
The soul treads on, both night and day,
In quest for light, truth's golden ray.

Through forests dark and mountains sheer,
Across the plains, far and near,
With every step, its purpose grows,
Amidst the thorns, a budding rose.

In temples old and valleys deep,
Where shadows dance and secrets keep,
The pilgrimage continues on,
From the first light to the last dawn.

In every heart, a sacred flame,
A desire to rise, to claim,
The journey is the soul's true test,
In seeking more, we find our rest.

To Sleep Under Strange Stars

Beneath a sky not mine to claim,
Where constellations hold no name,
I lay my weary head to rest,
In lands afar, a questing guest.

The moon's soft glow on foreign lands,
Speaks gently of unseen hands,
That guide my dreams across the seas,
To sleep under strange stars, at ease.

The night air whispers tales of old,
Of adventurers bold and stories untold,
Under these heavens, vast and wide,
I find a place to hide, inside.

With each new dawn, I rise anew,
Embracing skies of endless hue,
To sleep under strange stars, a balm,
In the night's vast, peaceful calm.

Beyond Familiar Horizons

Beyond the hills that hem my heart,
Where dreams and daylights drift apart,
The call of wild, unknown spaces,
Urges me to distant places.

Past the fields, where children play,
Into the embrace of the fray,
I chase the sun, its fading light,
Guides me through the coming night.

With every step, a new scene unfurls,
Amongst the clouds, my spirit twirls,
Beyond familiar horizons, I roam,
In search of truth, in search of home.

The world, a tapestry so wide,
In every thread, a secret hides,
Beyond familiar horizons, I see,
The person that I yearn to be.

The Call of Distant Shores

The ocean wind, so wild and free,
Calls out to the soul in me,
To leave behind the shore's safe ground,
For distant lands where hope is found.

Across the waves, under open skies,
Where the horizon forever lies,
The call of distant shores, so sweet,
Makes my heart with excitement beat.

With sails unfurled, to the unknown,
Where seeds of dreams are sown,
Distant shores with stories new,
Await my touch, my view.

Each wave that crashes, each gull that flies,
Tells of lands beyond the skies,
The call of distant shores, a song,
Of where my heart truly belongs.

Trailing the Stars

In the silence of the night, under the dim moonlight,
We trail the stars, in their endless flight.
Across the canvas of the sky, vast and wide,
The dreams of wanderers and poets coincide.

With every step, myths and constellations unfold,
Telling tales of the brave, the bashful, and the bold.
In the whisper of the cosmos, we find our guide,
Leading us on a journey, where our fears collide.

Through the silence of the universe, so profound,
The stars narrate stories without a sound.
In their light, we discover truths untold,
A celestial path for our dreams to behold.

In the vastness above, we drift and dance,
With stars that lead us into a trance.
Their glow, a beacon in the night's embrace,
Guides us back to hope, a familiar place.

Odyssey of the Ever-restless

Upon the waves of change, we set our sails,
An odyssey of the ever-restless prevails.
Seeking horizons where the sun meets the sea,
We journey forth, bound by the quest to be free.

Through storms and calm, under the canopy of stars,
We navigate the map drawn in our scars.
Every wave a lesson, every gale a test,
In the heart of the ocean, we find our quest.

Islands of dreams dot the sprawling blue,
Each a promise of a start anew.
We anchor in bays, where stories entwine,
In search of treasures, both tangible and divine.

With each landfall, our spirits soar,
Yet the sea calls us back, forevermore.
Bound to the tide, like the moon to the night,
We sail on, in the ever-restless fight.

Veins of the Earth

Beneath the surface, a world unseen,
Where the roots of the Earth hold secrets, keen.
Through the veins of the world, life pulses strong,
In the silent depths, where shadows belong.

Rivers of stone, and mountains deep,
Hold the mysteries that the earth does keep.
In the heart of the darkness, gems glimmer bright,
A testament to the Earth's concealed might.

The roots of trees, like fingers, spread,
Touching the essence of the dead.
They drink from the wells of ancient lore,
Bringing life to the world, evermore.

In the silent caverns, where time stands still,
Nature carves her story, with iron will.
In the veins of the Earth, we find our kin,
Connected to the world, from without and within.

Walking with Shadows

In the twilight hours, when daylight fades,
We walk with shadows, through the glades.
Hand in hand with the ghosts of the past,
In the silence, our fears are cast.

With each step, the shadows dance,
Mirroring our every glance.
In their silent company, we do not walk alone,
For in the shadows, forgotten tales are shown.

Through the darkened streets and alleyways dim,
The whispers of history, a haunting hymn.
The shadows, keepers of secrets untold,
Guard the mysteries that the night does hold.

As dawn approaches, the shadows wane,
Yet in our hearts, they forever remain.
For in the dance with shadows, we find,
A reflection of the thoughts within our mind.

Paths Woven of Sunsets

Upon the tapestry of dusk, colors weave,
With every thread, a dreamer's heart believes.
Through the loom of clouds, the sun takes leave,
In the masterpiece, a silent sigh heaves.

The horizon blushes in hues so bold,
A path unwinds where stories will be told.
Onwards, where the sky meets sea, untold,
Under the canvas, our spirits unfold.

Each step bathed in the fading light,
Guided by the promise of the night.
Our path woven of sunsets, a sight,
Carries us softly into the twilight.

At the Edge of Discovery

At the world's end, where the unknown calls,
Eyes glisten with dreams, on the edge, we stand.
With every fear that into the abyss falls,
A step forward taken, into the new land.

Beyond the maps, where the sea meets the sky,
Lies the beauty that beckons us to fly.
On this precipice, where our fates tie,
We leap, embracing what lives doth imply.

In the heart of the storm, where truths hide,
Thunder speaks, and in its voice, we confide.
With every bolt, our fears are defied,
At the edge of discovery, we stride.

Nomad's Chronicles

Across the deserts of time, I roam,
Each grain of sand, a story untold.
Underneath the star's eternal dome,
I find the tales of ancients, bold.

With every dawn, my journey renews,
Horizons whisper of the ways to tread.
In the silence, my soul pursues,
The wisdom in the wind, unsaid.

Through the valleys and over the hills,
In search of the essence of truth.
The spirit of the earth, my heart fills,
With every step, the zeal of youth.

As the moon ascends, I lay to rest,
In the lap of the earth, I find my quest.
By the stories of fire, I am blessed,
In the nomad's chronicles, my soul is dressed.

Beyond the Next Horizon

Beyond the next horizon, what waits?
A realm untouched by time or trial.
Each dawn, an invitation that satiates,
The thirst for discovery, mile after mile.

Over the mountains, across the seas,
Beyond the veil of the morning mist,
Our hearts yearn for the embrace of these,
Unseen worlds, by the sun's first kiss.

The journey is long, the path unclear,
But driven by the quest for the unknown.
The horizon calls, and we draw near,
In its mystery, our future is shown.

With every ending, a beginning anew,
The horizon beckons, a challenge, a clue.
In the quest beyond, our spirits renew,
Onward we travel, to dreams that ensue.

Drifter's Dream

Beneath the canvas of starlit skies,
A drifter dreams with open eyes.
Fields of wonder, streams so bright,
He traverses lands in the quiet of night.

Over mountains draped in snow,
Through valleys where wild rivers flow.
He seeks the tales yet untold,
In his heart, the world he holds.

Moonlight whispers through the trees,
The drifter moves with silent ease.
Every step, a story new,
Under the vast, embracing blue.

With each dawn, his dream anew,
Horizons vast, and skies so blue.
His spirit free, in endless roam,
The earth beneath, forever home.

Tales of joy and sorrow blend,
Journeys start where trails end.
In dreams, he finds what awake he seeks,
The strength of mountains, the peace of creeks.

Wandering Where the Wind Blows

I wander where the wild wind blows,
Across the fields, where nobody knows.
The whispers in the air so light,
Guide me through the day and night.

The rustle of leaves, the dance of the trees,
My heart alight, my soul at ease.
Footsteps tread on paths unseen,
Following where the wind has been.

The world unfolds in hues so bright,
Under the sun, stars, and moonlight.
Journeys taken, stories sewn,
In every whisper, the wind has blown.

Through storms and calm, its voice rings true,
A guide, a friend, in skies so blue.
With every breath, the world anew,
I wander where the wind whispers through.

My path, a series of fleeting traces,
Leading to uncharted places.
With the wind, my relentless guide,
In its embrace, I forever glide.

Roaming the Realms Unseen

In realms unseen, where shadows dance,
   I roam the void, I take my chance.
   Between the whispers of the night,
  I seek the truths hidden from sight.

  Through the veil of mystery deep,
  Past the guardians of secrets keep.
  I wander realms, both dark and fair,
    Seeking answers, everywhere.

Where light and shadow intertwine,
  In the silence of the crypts, I find.
  The echoes of the ancient ones,
   Whispers of times long gone.

With every step, the unseen clearer,
The distant realms drawing nearer.
The mysteries of the dark embrace,
   In the quiet, I find my place.

This journey through the night, alone,
Where every shadow's a stepping stone.
Roaming through the unseen, I strive,
   In the mysteries, I come alive.

The Quest for Distant Echoes

In search of echoes from afar,
I travel under the evening star.
Through forests dark and valleys deep,
The secrets of the ancient, I seek.

Over craggy hills and waters wide,
On this quest, I will not be denied.
The whispers of the past call my name,
In the search for echoes, a silent flame.

Across the lands, through the mists of time,
I listen for the ancient chime.
The song of stars, the dance of the moon,
In the quiet night, I'm attuned.

With every echo that I chase,
I find the traces of a hidden grace.
The remnants of a world so vast,
In these echoes, the future's cast.

This journey through time and space,
A quest for echoes, a relentless chase.
With every discovery, my heart grows fonder,
On this path, I shall always wander.

The Soul's Yearning Journey

In depths of night, stars whisper to the soul,
Guiding through the dark, where dreams often stroll.
A quest for meaning, beyond the mundane role,
Yearning for a sign, to mend and make whole.

With every sunrise, hopes anew take flight,
Chasing horizons, where day kisses night.
The soul's journey, a path beyond mere sight,
Seeking its echo in the soft twilight.

Through valleys deep, where shadows hold sway,
And mountain peaks, where the heavens play,
The journey's map, written in the heart's fray,
Guides the soul onward, come what may.

In every tear, a lesson to be learned,
In every smile, a victory earned.
The soul's yearning journey, ardently yearned,
Toward the light of truth, forever turned.

Songs of the Wayward Traveler

Upon roads less traveled, the wayward goes,
Wandering beneath the moon's gentle throes.
With a heart full of songs, no end foreknows,
Each step a note, in the night it bestows.

The world's vast wonders, through the traveler's eyes,
Mountains, rivers, under the endless skies.
Each song a memory, where heart lies,
In every verse, a piece of wisdom defies.

Through storms and calm, the melody plays on,
Echoing the spirit of dawn.
Songs of joy, sorrow, of being withdrawn,
In the traveler's heart, they're never gone.

With every journey, the traveler finds,
A tune anew, in the world's binds.
Songs of the wayward, through trials and binds,
A symphony that forever reminds.

Seeking the World's Secrets

Curiosity, like a boundless sea,
Drives the mind to explore, wild and free.
Hidden truths, in the world's vast decree,
Seeking secrets, where they may be.

Beneath the soil, and above the clouds,
In silent whispers, and in crowds loud.
The quest for knowledge, breaking all shrouds,
To uncover, what the world allows.

Through ancient texts and ruins old,
In whispered legends, and tales bold.
The secrets of the world, slowly unfold,
In the seeker's heart, they take hold.

With every discovery, a new mystery,
In the world's secrets, an endless history.
Seeking not for glory, nor for victory,
But for the truth, in its raw simplicity.

Footsteps Across the Forgotten

Through lands untouched, and paths overgrown,
Where echoes of the past, softly moan.
Footsteps wander, into the unknown,
Seeking places, the world has outshone.

Ancient stones, with stories untold,
Forests whispering tales, bold and old.
The forgotten, their beauty behold,
In their silence, a wonder to unfold.

Through forgotten gates, and fallen walls,
Where history's whisper, softly calls.
Each step, a journey through time enthralls,
Unveiling secrets, as night befalls.

In the forgotten, a charm resides,
A testament of time, that still abides.
Across these lands, the wanderer strides,
Where the essence of history, in silence, hides.

Far Beyond Familiar Shores

O'er seas that stretch far beyond gaze,
Where mysteries lie deep and profound,
Beneath the sun's eternal blaze,
Lies tales untold, in whispers sound.

Upon waves that dance with grace,
Carrying dreams to distant lands,
Each crest a fleeting, tender embrace,
Crafted by time's unseen hands.

Horizon meets the sky in kiss,
Where blues of every shade converge,
In such vast space, do souls reminisce,
As past and future surge.

Ships that journey through the night,
Guided by the stars' soft glow,
Within them burns a hopeful light,
Far beyond familiar shores, they go.

Amidst the Whispering Sands

In lands where silence reigns as king,
And sands that whisper ancient tales,
The wind's soft hymn begins to sing,
O'er dunes and vast, empty vales.

Beneath the sun's relentless reign,
Lie secrets buried, time-encased,
Awaiting rain's forgiving bane,
In eternity's embrace, they're laced.

Through day and night, the earth does speak,
In tongues lost to man's memory,
Its voice a beacon, strong yet meek,
Within the desert's boundless sea.

Eternal sands, with whispers sown,
Chart the tales of whence we came,
In grains of truth, the past is shown,
Each particle a fleeting flame.

Under the Moon's Silent Watch

Beneath the moon's unwavering gaze,
Where shadows dance in twilight's blend,
Through the silent night, our spirits daze,
In worlds where time does seem to bend.

The silver light that softly falls,
Illuminates the paths unknown,
Guiding travelers through night's halls,
Where seeds of dreams are gently sown.

In quietude does beauty thrive,
Under the watchful eye above,
Where secrets of the night revive,
In the silent kingdom of the dove.

As stars tiptoe across the sky,
Whispering tales of ages old,
Under the moon, we softly sigh,
In its embrace, we find our hold.

Paths Woven of Sunsets

Within the glow of fading light,
Where day and night in brief, sweet kiss,
Colors blend in soft delight,
Fashioning a path of bliss.

Skies painted with a master's hand,
In strokes of pink, and gold, and blue,
Lead to the heart's hidden land,
Where every whispered dream rings true.

Upon this road of shifting hue,
With steps as light as evening's breath,
Each moment feels tender and new,
A dance with joy, bereft of death.

Into the sunset's embrace we merge,
With hearts aglow and eyes wide shut,
The horizon beckons, a song to urge,
Paths woven of sunsets, forever cut.

A Tapestry of Trails

In woven paths of verdant thread,
Through whispering woods and fields spread,
Each trail a tale, a journey's lead,
To where earth's silent secrets tread.

Beneath the sun, under the moon's gaze,
Across the streams that softly blaze,
Hills and valleys, in the dawn's haze,
A tapestry of trails, an endless maze.

Footsteps echo, the only sound,
In nature's cathedral, vast and profound,
Where thoughts and dreams are unbound,
And the spirit's true course is found.

Through seasons' change and time's flow,
Along these paths, the heart will know,
With every step, the soul will grow,
On the tapestry of trails, where wanderers go.

Under the Spell of the Horizon

Beneath the canvas vast and wide,
Where sky and earth in blue collide,
Eyes gaze afar, in wonder, tied,
Under the spell of the horizon, we abide.

Each morning's glow, each evening's fade,
In shades of amber, gold, and jade,
The horizon whispers, softly bade,
Of distant dreams not yet played.

Across the oceans, over the sands,
The horizon beckons, with unseen hands,
To follow where the sky commands,
In pursuit of mysteries that no map lands.

With hearts as compass, we embark,
Towards that line where adventures spark,
Beyond the light and past the dark,
Under the spell of the horizon, we make our mark.

In the quiet moments, when thoughts are clear,
The horizon calls, pulls us near,
A promise of journeys, far and dear,
Under its spell, we cast away fear.

Discoveries Beyond the Veil

In realms unseen, where shadows dance,
And whispered secrets take their stance,
Beyond the veil, we take our chance,
To unlock the universe's grand expanse.

Through the mist of mystery's embrace,
Past the edge of time and space,
Where light and darkness interlace,
Discoveries beyond the veil we face.

With eyes open to the unseen,
In places where few have been,
The essence of what lies between,
Reveals a world, pristine and keen.

In every star's distant glow,
In every seed that fate may sow,
There lies a truth, for us to know,
Beyond the veil, where wonders flow.

So let us venture, bold and brave,
Across the boundaries of the grave,
In pursuit of the knowledge we crave,
Discoveries beyond the veil, forever our enclave.

Yearning for the Yonder

With eyes cast towards the distant lands,
A heart that beats, and dreams that stands,
In every soul, an explorer expands,
Yearning for the yonder, with outstretched hands.

Beyond the mountains, across the seas,
Where winds whisper secrets through the trees,
The spirit wanders, forever seeks,
The yonder calls, and the heart leaps.

In pursuit of landscapes, unknown and vast,
Where future's stories eclipse the past,
Our yearnings guide us, sails to mast,
Towards the yonder, boundless and vast.

Under the stars, beneath the sun,
From dawn till dusk, our quest begun,
The yearning for the yonder, never done,
Until the world and our hearts are one.

So we journey, with hope in our song,
Believing the yonder is where we belong,
In the quest for the distant, we find we're strong,
Yearning for the yonder, pushing us along.

Into the Arms of the Unknown

Beyond the edge of certainty, we tread,
Where every whisper feels like thunder's roar.
Into the arms of the unknown, we're led,
By dreams that beckon from a distant shore.

With every step, the ground gives way to air,
The familiar fades, and new realms arise.
In the heart of mystery, stripped bare,
We find the truth that underlies the skies.

Fear not the darkness nor the steep descent,
For in the void, the stars begin to dance.
Embrace the unknown with pure intent,
And in its depths, you'll find a second chance.

Unknown roads stretch out with promise vast,
In their shadows, our former selves are cast.

With courage, we claim the future from the past,
Into the arms of the unknown, at last.

Chasing Shadows Across the World

In the light of a setting sun, we chase,
Shadows that stretch and intertwine with fate.
Across the world, a fleeting, silent race,
In pursuit of dreams that can't wait.

Through cities that pulse with life's refrain,
Over mountains crowned with snow and awe.
Chasing shadows, we seek to explain,
The mysteries that through the ages gnaw.

Across deserts where the stars align,
Under seas where silent whispers flow.
In shadows, truths and dreams intertwine,
Revealing ways we must come to know.

Yet, in our quest, a greater truth we find,
Within our hearts, shadows and light combined.

In every shadow, a new path unwinds,
Across the world, our spirits intertwined.

The Whispering Gallery of the Earth

Beneath the canopy of ancient trees,
A whisper carries on the morning breeze.
The Earth herself speaks in hushed tones,
Her secrets buried under stones.

In every leaf, a story told,
Of cycles new and epochs old.
The whispering gallery, wide and vast,
Speaks of the future, present, past.

The wind's soft murmur, a symphony,
Composed by nature's pure alchemy.
It tells of days when the Earth was young,
And of the many songs yet unsung.

Listen close and you may hear,
The Earth's soft whisper in your ear.

In this gallery, where whispers flow,
We find connection, peace, and woe.

Ascending the Peaks of Imagination

Upon the wings of thought, we soar above,
Ascending peaks of sheer imagination.
Each height surpassed reveals new heights to love,
In realms bound only by our own creation.

Through valleys deep where shadowed mysteries dwell,
Over rivers of crystal-clear insight.
Our imaginations, a powerful spell,
Turning darkest fears into brightest light.

With every peak, a broader view unfolds,
Horizons stretch; endless skies invite.
Each journey filled with stories yet untold,
On paths illuminated by inner light.

So let us climb, with hearts open and free,
Upon the peaks of what we dare to be.

Imagination's landscape, wide and vast,
Within it, the blueprint of futures cast.

Through the Veil of Distant Thunders

Through skies, where distant thunders roar,
We seek the light, the open pour,
A quest through night's embracing chains,
Where silence sings the sweetest strains.

Beyond the veil, where shadows blend,
Our hearts, with the universe, mend,
Each flash reveals a hidden door,
To worlds unseen, forevermore.

The tempest's heart, so wild and free,
Echoes the soul's deep mystery,
Within its core, the truth we find,
A bond with the eternal mind.

Through storms, we sail towards the dawn,
The veil of night, at last, withdrawn,
In the silence, after the thunder's cry,
Lies the path where our spirits fly.

Footprints on the Path Unknown

On paths unkown, beneath the sky's vast dome,
We walk, where others fear to roam,
Each footprint marks a story untold,
A quest for the brave, the fearless, bold.

The journey's call, so clear and deep,
Awakens the soul from its ancient sleep,
With every step, the unknown greets,
In its mystery, our heart beats.

Unseen trails, where secrets hide,
In shadows, our true selves abide,
With courage, we face the untamed land,
Guided by an unseen hand.

The path unknown, with its twists and turns,
Teaches lessons we are here to learn,
In every footprint, left behind,
A piece of us, the world will find.

Drifting on the Tides of Fate

Upon the tides of fate, we're cast,
The future blurred, the past is vast,
Drifting on this ceaseless sea,
We seek what is and what might be.

Each wave a choice, each current, a path,
We navigate the aftermath,
In the ocean wide, under stars above,
We sail on hope, and dreams of love.

The water whispers secrets old,
Of destinies untold, bold,
In its depths, truths lie hidden,
In its song, our fears unbidden.

With sails unfurled to the unknown,
We face the storm, we face alone,
Yet in the heart, where dreams reside,
Is where our true north lies, our guide.

Adrift, yet not without our will,
On these tides, our dreams fulfill,
Each moment a step towards our fate,
Guided by love, steered by the wait.

Quest for the Unseen World

In search of realms that lie unseen,
Beyond the grasp of where we've been,
We venture forth, with hearts aglow,
To lands mysterious, we yearn to know.

Through forests deep and mountains high,
Underneath the boundless sky,
Our spirits quest, our souls aspire,
To reach the heights, ever higher.

The unseen world, with wonders rife,
A tapestry of mystery and life,
Calls to the heart that seeks to find,
The truths that lie deeply entwined.

With every step, the path unfolds,
A story new, as old as old,
The quest for knowledge, for insight,
Leads us through the day and night.

Within the heart, the unseen world dwells,
A realm where profound wisdom tells,
Of a journey not just of the feet,
But of the soul, where two worlds meet.

The Heart's Unquenched Thirst

In the silence of the night, under star's watchful glow,
A heart whispers secrets only the moon will know.
Dreams of love unfulfilled, a melody unsung,
An unquenched thirst within, since time was young.

Through the endless days and into the despair of night,
It searches for solace, for a spark of light.
In the laughter of the rain, in the tear's silent fall,
The heart seeks its other, its soul's eternal call.

Among crowded paths or in solitude's embrace,
It wanders, yearns for a glimpse of grace.
The touch of another, in whose eyes it will drown,
To quench its thirst, in love's profound.

In dreams, it soars high, beyond the realm of pain,
Believing in a world where love will reign.
Yet, awake, it finds itself tethered, alone,
Thirsting still, in the dark, unknown.

Beyond the Last Blue Mountain

Beyond the last blue mountain, under the wide, infinite sky,
Lies a land of dreams, where hopes never die.
The journey's long, the paths untread,
But hearts brave the unknown, by desire and wonder led.

Through mists that cling and whispers of the old,
The bold trek onward, with spirits uncontrolled.
Over peaks touching the heavens, through valleys deep and wide,
In search of the land beyond, where peace and dreams reside.

On this quest, weary souls may falter, may fall,
Yet, the mountain's call, to them still all.
It sings of freedom, of adventures untold,
Beckoning the brave, the young, and the old.

When the last summit's conquered, and the tired eyes see,
The land beyond the blue mountain, majestic and free.
There, beneath the endless skies, they'll find,
The tranquility and joy that once was a mere whisper in the mind.

In Quest of the Sunset's Fire

With hearts ablaze and eyes wide, we chase the dying light,
In quest of the sunset's fire, before the fall of night.
The horizon calls, its colors bold and bright,
A fleeting beauty, in its final, glorious sight.

The sun dips lower, setting the sky aflame,
In hues of orange and red, never twice the same.
Every step forward, in anticipation we take,
For a glimpse of magic, for our dreaming hearts' sake.

Through fields of gold, and shadows long,
We follow the fiery trail, our spirits strong.
The end seems near, yet always just out of reach,
A lesson in desire, the sunset's fire does teach.

As darkness veils the sky, and the stars above ignite,
We stand in silent awe, of the day's last light.
Though the sunset's fire dims, in our hearts it will reside,
A memory bright, of the journey, of the pride.

The Long Road to Nowhere's End

On the long road to nowhere's end, we walk in solitude,
A journey without a destination, a path without latitude.
With each step forward, the past fades away,
Into the embrace of the unknown, we sway.

The road stretches on, under skies ever-changing,
Through landscapes of memories, endlessly ranging.
No maps to guide us, no stars to steer by,
Just the road, the journey, and the vast, open sky.

We seek not arrival, for the journey itself is the goal,
A pilgrimage of the spirit, a test of the soul.
The road teaches lessons of loss, love, and discovery,
In the quiet moments, we find ourselves, and recovery.

Though the road to nowhere's end may be long and alone,
It's filled with the beauty of the world unknown.
And at the end, when we finally rest,
We'll know we've lived, we've journeyed, we've quested.

Sailing the Seas of the Unfound

Upon a ship of dreams and wonder, we set sail,
Across the seas where mysteries unveil.
Guided by stars, the night's gentle gown,
In search of lands that maps do not down.

Beneath the moon's watchful, silvery eye,
The waves whisper tales, old as the sky.
Holding secrets, in depths unseen,
Sailing the seas of the unfound, serene.

The breeze sings of places, untouched, so fair,
Where sunlight dances through the crisp, clear air.
Horizons blend where the sea meets the sky,
A canvas of beauty, vast and shy.

With hearts as our compass, wild and free,
We voyage on, boundless, like the sea.
Beyond the edge of the world, we roam,
In search of the unfound, where dreams call home.

Glimpses of Paradise Lost

In gardens where once immortality bloomed,
Now silence and shadows have loomed.
Trees whisper of glory, now gone,
In echoes of paradise, withdrawn.

Beneath the boughs, where light gently sifts,
Lies the memory of Eden, as time drifts.
Flowers weep, their colors fade,
In the remnants of the paradise that once swayed.

Rivers mourn as they flow,
Through lands where milk and honey no longer grow.
The earth holds tight, its secrets buried deep,
Of a paradise lost, in its eternal sleep.

Yet, in the heart, a glow remains,
A hope that whispers, amidst the pains.
For every dusk, there's a dawn's light,
In glimpses of paradise, lost from sight, yet bright.

Towards the Realm of Endless Day

Beyond the night, a realm awaits,
Where dawn holds the gates.
Here, in the endless day,
Dreams find their way.

No shadow falls, no night can stay,
In lands where light and hope play.
Souls soar, free of their weight,
Towards the dawn, through the golden gate.

Stars guide us on this journey afar,
Illuminating the path, from night to star.
In visions of what might be,
We travel, hearts unchained and free.

Endless day, where love resides,
In the realm where truth abides.
Towards this light, we yearn to stray,
On paths illuminated by eternal day.

Among the Ruins of Yesterdays

Among the ruins of yesterdays,
Where the echo of past laughter plays.
Memories like vines, entwine,
Among the wreckage of the divine.

Walls that once stood tall and proud,
Now whisper stories, once loud.
Through this desolation, beauty grows,
A testament to time, it shows.

Here, in the remnants of dreams,
Underneath the moon's gentle beams.
Lie secrets, waiting to be found,
In the silence, there's a profound sound.

Each stone a story, a memory vested,
In ruins, history is nested.
Among these echoes, we understand,
The fleeting moment of time's sand.

Through the Gateway of Forgotten Kings

In ruins old where whispers cling,
Beneath the moon's forlorn sing,
Through the gateway of forgotten kings,
    Time itself unfurls its wings.

Where shadows merge with ancient stories,
The mossy stones guard hidden glories,
Silent echoes of majestic might,
    In the quiet depth of night.

Through arches tall and splendor faded,
By countless seasons softly jaded,
The air is thick with tales untold,
    In the land where kings of old.

Marched with pride under starry veils,
Their legends now but ghostly tales,
Through the gateway, history springs,
    In the realm of forgotten kings.

The Eternal Itinerant's Soliloquy

With every sunrise, my journey anew,
Across horizons where the wild winds blew,
The eternal itinerant, bound by no ties,
Finding solace beneath the sprawling skies.

Through cities and valleys, mountains and plains,
Each step a story, in my heart remains,
A soliloquy of freedom, whispered to the breeze,
Carried over oceans, through forests and seas.

Not for me the anchor, nor the harbor's call,
The world is my canvas, and I must paint it all,
With hues of adventure, in shades of dawn and dusk,
Each stroke a memory, in the air, a musk.

The road stretches endless, under the celestial sphere,
In the itinerant's heart, there's no room for fear,
For every destination offers its unique solace,
In the eternal journey, I find my true oasis.

Dancing in the Courts of Chaos

In the labyrinth where shadows play,
And the laws of nature gently fray,
Dancing in the courts of chaos, we sway,
To the music that the wild winds convey.

Beneath the cloak of the swirling night,
Where stars are shaken from their height,
We find a rhythm, pure and right,
In the heart of darkness, our souls ignite.

The melody, a tempest's roar,
On this untamed dance floor,
Each step, a defiance at its core,
In chaos, our spirits soar.

With every turn, a new world born,
In the eye of the storm, we're torn,
Yet in tumult, we find our form,
Dancing where others might mourn.

In this court where chaos reigns,
Freedom and frenzy, with no chains,
Here, our essence truly gains,
In the hurricane's veins, our dance remains.

The Vagabond's Infinite Canvas

Upon the road, under the sky's grand vast,
The vagabond finds the canvas so vast,
Each horizon, a stroke of paint anew,
In the gallery of the wind, where dreams brew.

With every dawn, a new masterpiece begins,
Rivers shimmer as the world softly spins,
Mountains rise, in hues of earth and stone,
Under the wanderer's gaze, they stand alone.

The forests whisper in shades of green,
A sight so serene, hardly ever seen,
Skies bleed at dusk, in colors so bold,
The canvas alive, as night unfolds.

In the vast gallery of wild open space,
The vagabond moves at their own pace,
With each step, the earth's stories unfurl,
On the infinite canvas, their path does swirl.

The journey never ends, the trail winds on,
From the break of each dawn to the dusk's yawn,
The world's beauty, an endless mural sublime,
On this infinite canvas, they dance through time.

Lost Among Stars

In heavens vast, where darkness reigns and glows,
    Beside the moons and suns that distant lie,
    A soul drifts, in the cosmic dance, it flows,
    Lost among stars that freckle the night sky.

It wanders through the constellations, drawn
    By whispers of the universe, so vast,
    In search of where its essence might have gone,
    Adrift in light-years, both future and past.

Amidst the celestial bodies' embrace,
    Its heart beats in sync with pulsars' distant drum,
    Each throb a step in an endless, boundless race,
    A journey through the cosmos, lonesome hum.

Yet in this void, where solitude might drown,
    The soul finds peace, in starlight, it is found.

A ballad of the cosmos, broad and deep,
    Lost among stars, where silent wonders sleep.

Swept Away by the Quest

Upon a path that winds and never ends,
A seeker strides, with purpose in each step,
Guided by dreams that the vast world extends,
In quest of mysteries, their heart has leapt.

They venture forth, through forests deep and wide,
O'er mountains tall and rivers dark and deep,
With nothing but their courage as their guide,
In search of secrets that the ages keep.

Each journey faced with perils, sharp and dire,
The questing soul, undaunted, marches on,
Their spirit kindled by an inner fire,
Illuminating the path they're drawn upon.

And when at last their weary feet do rest,
The quest remains, their heart's eternal quest.

A tale of ventures bold and spirits brave,
Swept away by the quest that fulfills and saves.

Voyages of the Spirit

Within the human heart, an ocean lies,
With waves that crash against the shores of doubt,
The spirit, a ship that sails under skies,
Where dreams and fears in storms and calm make out.

It journeys on, though tempests rage and roar,
Through seas of grief and isles of fleeting joy,
Each hardship faced, a lesson at its core,
In realms emotions craft but not destroy.

Beyond the horizon, where hopes may gleam,
The spirit seeks the lands not yet explored,
Driven by the strength of an inner dream,
A voyage through the soul's vast, uncharted fjord.

This journey of the heart, both harsh and kind,
Reveals the depths and heights of the human mind.

So sail on, spirit, through life's vast expanse,
In voyages where dreams and purpose dance.

Dreaming of the Road Not Taken.

In dreams, I walk a path that splits in twain,
Under the canopy of choices' shade,
The road not taken, a haunting refrain,
A symphony of what-ifs, softly played.

One path worn, familiar to my feet,
The other, lush with mystery's allure,
Each step upon it sings of incomplete,
Adventures that the heart can but implore.

How often do I ponder where they lead,
These roads diverged beneath time's ancient bough,
And in my dreams, it's there I plant the seed,
Of paths not chosen, yet entice me now.

So in the night, 'neath starlight's gentle gaze,
I dream of roads not taken, lost in haze.

A reflection deep, of choices unseen,
Dreaming of the road, of what might have been.

Through Lands of Lore

Across the verdant fields so wide,
Where tales and legends softly hide,
Beneath the glow of the twilight bower,
Lies the whisper of each ancient power.

Through forests deep and rivers clear,
Echoes of the past draw near,
In every stone and every leaf,
Lies a story of joy and grief.

O'er hills aglow with morning light,
And valleys shrouded in the night,
The lands of lore, with secrets untold,
Hold the tales of the brave and bold.

With every step upon this earth,
We tread on stories of death and birth,
The land beneath, the sky above,
Bind each soul in endless love.

So let us wander, let us roam,
Through lands of lore we call our home,
For in each tale and myth we find,
The journey of our own mankind.

Where Earth Meets Sky

At the horizon, where earth meets sky,
In the embrace of the dawn's early light,
Dreams take flight on wings so high,
And the world is reborn, pure and bright.

The sun kisses the mountaintop's cheek,
While rivers sing to valleys deep,
Each moment a new story to seek,
In this land where the earth and sky weep.

Beneath the expanse of the azure dome,
Lies the boundless heart of our roam,
The canvas of existence, finely spun,
Where our fates and the cosmos become one.

As dusk falls, and stars begin to show,
The night whispers secrets old and new,
In the sacred place where earth meets sky,
The soul finds tales as vast as the blue.

Let us find solace in this endless dance,
Of light and shadow, sun and moon's trance,
For at the place where earth meets sky,
Lies the horizon of our hopeful glance.

The Wanderer's Reflection

Upon the mirror of the tranquil lake,
Where silence whispers and the willows quake,
The wanderer sees not just his face,
But the reflection of his soul's embrace.

Through paths unknown and forests deep,
Where shadows dance and the mountains steep,
The journey taken, a tale to tell,
In the heart where true adventures dwell.

With each step upon the earth's broad back,
He learns the virtues that many lack,
Compassion, courage, and the love for all,
In every rise, and in every fall.

Reflecting on the miles left behind,
The wanderer seeks, yet what does he find?
A world within, vast and unexplored,
An endless quest for the heart's reward.

So let the wanderer's reflection show,
Not just a man, but the seeds he'll sow,
In the hearts of those whose paths he'll cross,
The memories of gains and of loss.

Embracing the Path of the Unknown

Into the veil of the unknown we tread,
With hearts aflame and spirits fed,
Leaving behind the familiar shore,
To embrace the mystery of what lies before.

Each step a leap in the vast expanse,
Guided by chance, or perhaps by lance,
In the path of the unknown, we find,
Our fears and hopes, intertwined.

The stars above, our ancient guide,
Illuminating the path, side by side,
Under their watch, we journey on,
Until the last trace of fear is gone.

With every breath, with every stride,
We conquer the unknown that resides,
Within the depths of our own soul,
On this journey, that makes us whole.

So let us embrace the path untrod,
The journey to the unknown, with awe to God,
For in the quest to find our way,
We uncover the light of our own day.

The World Through Nomad Eyes

Across the vast, unending sands,
I wander, bare, without any ties.
Each grain tells tales of far-off lands,
In a world wide open to nomad eyes.

Over mountains high and valleys deep,
Where the earth touches the sky,
In nature's secrets, quietly I creep,
Under the watchful stars so shy.

Through bustling markets, alive with sound,
Where stories and spices freely flow.
My heart beats with a rhythm, unbound,
With every face and shadow I grow.

Past ancient ruins, whispering tales of old,
To the breeze, I lend my ears.
The stories of love and heroes bold,
Echo through the chasm of years.

By the rivers that carve the earth,
Beneath the smile of the moon's glow,
I find a sense of unspoken worth,
As I blend with the world's slow flow.

A Heart Unbound

In the quiet of the breaking dawn,
Where thoughts and dreams collide,
I find the strength to carry on,
With a heart unbound and wide.

Through the tumult of the day's embrace,
Amidst the chaos, I find grace.
My soul a bird, the sky its space,
In flight, all fears and doubts erase.

Beneath the vast, embracing night,
Where stars whisper to the sea,
My heart, unchained, takes its flight,
On wings of purest liberty.

Against the shade, against the bind,
My spirit dances, light and free.
No chains of doubt can ever find
The heart that lives so boundlessly.

In every breath, a song anew,
A melody of freedom's call.
In every step, the world's hue,
A heart unbound, embracing all.

Echoes of Faraway Places

In the silence of the night,
Echoes of faraway places take flight.
Whispers of lands I've yet to see,
Call to my heart, wild and free.

Beneath the canvas of endless blue,
The wind carries tales, old and new.
Of emerald forests and oceans deep,
Their secrets in my dreams they seep.

The scent of rain on distant soil,
Brings whispers of struggle, love, and toil.
Stories of places, exotic and strange,
Through these echoes, my dreams range.

In every echo, a desire is born,
To roam the earth from dusk till morn.
To touch, to feel, to embrace it all,
Before the final shadows fall.

With each echo, I find my pace,
A wanderer in this vast embrace.
Drawn to the lull of faraway places,
I am a seeker of untouched spaces.

Drifting on the Winds of Change

Like a leaf upon the breeze,
Drifting through the endless skies,
I move where the winds of change please,
Underneath the wide-open eyes.

With every gust, a new path forms,
Twisting, turning, ever new.
Beyond the norm, outside the storms,
I find my strength, my aim true.

In the heart of change, a constant beat,
A rhythm hidden beneath the fray.
In its cadence, I find retreat,
And in its song, I find my way.

The winds of change, they call my name,
A whisper soft, a roaring flame.
With every change, I'm not the same,
In this vast, ever-shifting game.

As seasons pass and years fade,
I ride the winds, unafraid.
For in the heart of every change,
Lies a truth, forever unswayed.

Chasing Horizons

In the quiet dawn, where dreams are born,
And the sky stretches wide and far,
We chase the horizons, hearts adorned,
With the light of the morning star.

Through fields of gold, under azure skies,
Our spirits soar, wild and free.
Every sunrise, a new surprise,
In the chase, we find who we're meant to be.

The horizon calls, with its silent song,
A melody of undiscovered lands.
With every step, we grow strong,
As horizons shift like timeless sands.

In this chase, our dreams entwine,
With the endless sky and the rolling sea.
On this journey, we find a sign,
Of what it truly means to be free.

So let us chase, till the end of days,
Through storms and under starlit canopies.
For in the pursuit, our hearts blaze,
Chasing horizons, where our spirit flies.

On the Road to Anywhere

On the road to anywhere, we find our way,
Feet set upon paths where wild winds sway.
With every tide, and turn of the earth,
We seek the essence of our own rebirth.

No maps required, for the heart leads on,
Under the moon's glow and the pink of dawn.
With whispers of the old and calls of the new,
Every road taken splits our world in two.

The journey's allure lies in its unknown,
In every shadow and light that's shown.
Reveling in tales of lands vast and wide,
On the road to anywhere, our dreams collide.

With companions few or in solitude's embrace,
We traverse valleys deep and mountain's face.
The road stretches out, endless and clear,
On it, we confront our deepest fear.

On the road to anywhere, our spirits soar,
With each step taken, we open a new door.
It's not the destination but the memories we create,
On this road to anywhere, our adventures await.

Flowers Bloom for Travelers

Along paths untrodden and views unseen,
Where travelers' feet have scarcely been,
Flowers bloom in vibrant array,
Marking journeys in a silent display.

With every hue, a story told,
Of brave adventures and hearts bold.
Travelers wander, and flowers sway,
In a dance of nature, night and day.

By mountain pass and river's curve,
Flowers bloom, a visual reserve.
For those who seek the world's true face,
In nature's beauty, they find their grace.

These blooms speak in colors, wild and bright,
Guiding travelers by day and night.
A secret language, for those who roam,
Flowers bloom, calling wanderers home.

In every petal, a journey's breath,
A testament to life, and not of death.
For as flowers bloom, so do we,
Travelers in time, forever free.

Wild Hearts and Open Roads

With wild hearts and open roads before us,
We embark on journeys that implore us.
To seek the unknown, face the wind's embrace,
On open roads, we find our truest grace.

Each turn reveals a story untold,
Of lands majestic, of warmth and cold.
Our hearts beat in tune with the world's ageless song,
On these roads, with the wild, we belong.

The horizon calls, a distant flame,
For wild hearts, life is never the same.
The road unwinds under wheel and tread,
A tapestry of dreams in our heads.

Through valleys deep and mountains high,
The open road stretches, meeting the sky.
Our hearts, untamed, in freedom's pursuit,
Find solace in paths, ancient and mute.

So let us ride, with souls aflame,
On this journey, no two ever the same.
With wild hearts and open roads, we weave,
A story of adventure, in which we believe.

Voyages of the Restless Heart

Upon the endless sea, my heart does ride,
Guided by stars, in night's embracing cloak.
O'er waves of dreams, where thoughts and hopes collide,
In search of shores, where waking dreams evoke.

Beneath the moon's soft gaze, my spirit sails,
Across the darkened vast, to lands unknown.
Where whispered winds tell tales of ancient tales,
And seeds of restless quests are gently sown.

Each dawn, a promise of new lands to seek,
Horizons wide, and mysteries to unfold.
The heart's desires, in silent whispers, speak,
Of stories yet to write, and tales untold.

In every port, a part of me remains,
A memory, a moment caught in time.
Yet, restless heart, still hungering for gains,
Sets sail again, to new worlds, sublime.

Voyages of the restless heart, unbound,
By chains of fear, or doubt's relentless maze.
In every journey, every quest, is found,
The essence of our dreams, through endless days.

Across Uncharted Skies

With wings unfurled, across the dusk we fly,
Charting courses where no one's dared before.
Beneath us, worlds untouched by mortal eye,
Above, uncharted skies forevermore.

Through cosmic seas, where stars like lighthouses guide,
We voyage on, by galaxies embraced.
In the quiet of space, where secrets reside,
We find our solace, in the vast, untraced.

Our compass is the heart, our map, the stars,
In the tapestry of night, our dreams we sew.
Beyond the bonds of Earth, past Mars and Mars,
To celestial realms, our spirits tow.

Each nightfall brings a chance to soar anew,
Into the dark, where wonders never cease.
Across uncharted skies, in hues of blue,
We find in exploration, our peace.

With every journey, knowledge we amass,
In starlit oceans, depths we dare to dive.
Across uncharted skies, we boldly pass,
To keep the flame of curiosity alive.

Beneath Foreign Stars

Beneath a blanket, foreign stars alight,
I dream of worlds beyond my eyes' own reach.
Where constellations cast a different sight,
And unknown tales, the night skies gently teach.

With every star, a story yet untold,
Far from the warmth of my familiar sun.
Beneath these skies, my thoughts begin to mold,
Imagining the many races run.

The universe, a tapestry so vast,
Enchants my mind, and fills my heart with awe.
Beneath foreign stars, I find at last,
A sense of wonder, without flaw.

These celestial sights, though far and wide,
Connect us all, no matter where we dwell.
Under the same sky, just on different side,
In starlit nights, profound stories swell.

So here I stand, beneath the cosmic seas,
Feeling both insignificant and grand.
Beneath foreign stars, I find my peace,
A wanderer in this immense, splendid land.

In the Footsteps of Dawn

In the footsteps of dawn, I softly tread,
As the world awakes, in hues of gold and red.
Each morning's light, a canvas broad and bright,
Painting the day, after the long, dark night.

With every step, the world comes alive,
From the smallest bloom, to the busiest hive.
The chorus of birds, in the sky takes flight,
In the footsteps of dawn, the world's alight.

Across the fields, through forests deep and wide,
I wander free, with dawn as my guide.
The misty veils of night, they slowly fade,
Revealing the beauty, the night had made.

Through this journey, I learn, I see, I grow,
Following the light, wherever it may go.
In the footsteps of dawn, my fears allayed,
By the promise of new light, new paths laid.

As day takes hold, and shadows retreat,
The cycle of life, once more, complete.
In the footsteps of dawn, my soul feels drawn,
To the endless beauty, of each breaking dawn.

Echoes of Forgotten Trails

Whispers linger in the ancient trees,
Trails lost to time, to dust, to breeze.
Echoes of footprints, silent and deep,
Carry secrets that the shadows keep.

Veins of the earth, worn by restless feet,
Paths that witnessed victories and defeat.
Each stone, a story; each turn, a tale,
In the silence, past whispers prevail.

Leaves rustle with the sound of yore,
Guiding travelers to a timeless shore.
The wind hums a melody, old and frail,
A song of journeys on forgotten trails.

Through the mists of time, visions unfurl,
Where the past and present softly swirl.
Echoes of forgotten trails, forever pale,
In the heart of the wild, they softly hail.

Time marches on, relentless and bold,
Yet these ancient paths, in memory, hold.
A testament to the days long gone,
In echoes of forgotten trails, life goes on.

Boundless as the Starlit Sky

Above, a canvas vast and wide,
The starlit sky, in glory, pride.
Glimmers of eternity dance in the night,
A spectacle of cosmos, an endless flight.

In the quiet of darkness, whispers soar,
Tales of the universe, myths of yore.
Each star, a beacon in the boundless blue,
A dream, a wish, a hope anew.

Boundless as the starlit sky,
Where dreams take wing, and spirits fly.
In the silence of the cosmos, peace is found,
Amidst the stars, our thoughts unbound.

Infinite worlds, beyond our sight,
Glow in the harmony of celestial light.
A symphony of the cosmos, vast and free,
In the starlit sky, we find infinity.

Under the dome of the night so grand,
Hand in hand, on this earth, we stand.
Gazing up at the universe, wild and shy,
Our spirits boundless, as the starlit sky.

By the Light of Wandering Stars

By the light of wandering stars, we tread,
Paths unveiled, where few have led.
Guided by the whispers of the night,
In the darkness, we find our light.

Through the veil of shadows, quietly we roam,
Under the gaze of celestial dome.
Wandering stars, in the silence, speak,
Of mysteries ancient, of futures bleak.

With each step, a story unfolds,
Beneath the stars, the earth gently holds.
A journey taken, a destiny embraced,
By the light of wandering stars, we're graced.

Amidst the tapestry of the cosmic sea,
We find solace, we find the key.
In the gentle glow of night's embrace,
By wandering stars, we find our place.

Through the aeons, as ages pass,
Our spirits roam, free at last.
By the light of wandering stars, so far,
We navigate, by the celestial spar.

Shadows in the Valley of the Unknown

In the valley of the unknown, shadows creep,
Where secrets lie in wait, buried deep.
A realm of whispers, of echoes unheard,
The line between the real and the absurd.

Through the mists, figures unseen,
Dance in the twilight, in a world in between.
Shadows stretch, reaching out wide,
In the valley, secrets and fates collide.

In the heart of darkness, fear takes hold,
Tales of the unknown, silently told.
The shadows play, in this eerie land,
Shapes shifting like grains of sand.

But even in the darkness, there is light,
A glimmer of hope, piercing the night.
In the shadows, we may find,
Answers to the questions that plague our mind.

So, in the valley of the unknown, we tread,
With courage in our heart, and no dread.
For in the shadows, truth is sown,
In the journey through the unknown.

The Eternal Search for Elsewhere

In realms of dream and shadow's fane,
We chase the sun, we court the rain.
Each step a story, old yet new,
In the eternal search for what is true.

Beyond the silvered veil of night,
Our souls take flight, in endless plight.
The heart yearns for unseen shores,
In the eternal search for something more.

Through whispering winds, our spirits soar,
Seeking the key to the unopened door.
A promise of wonder, a hint of lore,
In the eternal search, forevermore.

With each dawn, our hopes reborn,
In golden fields, 'neath skies adorned.
A tale of journeys, myth and mirth,
In the eternal search for our own earth.

On paths untrodden, 'neath stars unseen,
We find the spaces between the green.
A quest for peace, for love's embrace,
In the eternal search for our true place.

Skies Call to the Adventurous

Upon the wings of dawn, they ride,
Skies call to the brave, wide and wide.
The horizon beckons, a beckoning tide,
In skies that call, their hearts confide.

With every hue of the morning light,
They seek the edges of day and night.
A canvas of dreams in azure sight,
Skies call to the souls alight.

Through storms and whispers of clouds in flight,
They chase the whispers of the wind's might.
A covenant with the sky, a silent rite,
In skies that call, their fate takes flight.

Amidst the ballet of stars at night,
Adventurers dance in the moon's soft light.
A world unbound, limitless and bright,
Skies call to the seekers of height.

In the embrace of the infinite blue,
A promise of mysteries, old and new.
With hearts unchained, and eyes that pursue,
Skies call to the adventurous, ever true.

Over Mountains, Through Valleys

Over mountains high, where eagles dare,
We tread paths unseen, through thinning air.
The summit's call, so raw and rare,
Over mountains, our spirits bare.

Through valleys deep, where shadows play,
We find our solace, we find our way.
The earth's embrace, night and day,
Through valleys, our fears allay.

Crossing rivers, under starlit skies,
Witness to the world, through ancient eyes.
Each step a story, where truth never dies,
Over mountains, through valleys, our spirit flies.

Past hidden glens, where legends dwell,
We journey through our own story to tell.
A quest for beauty, a magic spell,
Over mountains, through valleys, we ring the bell.

With every peak, a new horizon seen,
Through every gorge, a fresh, verdant green.
A world of wonders, where we've never been,
Over mountains, through valleys, to the unseen.

Enchanted by the Roads Less Traveled

Enchanted by the roads less traveled,
Where mysteries and dreams are unraveled.
Each turn a story, under stars spangled,
On paths uncharted, our lives entangled.

Through forests deep, where whispers wait,
We chart our course, we tempt our fate.
In the silence of the woods, both early and late,
Enchanted roads call, at destiny's gate.

Across sands time-lost, under suns that burn,
Our hearts wander, at each twist and turn.
For the magic of the road, we eternally yearn,
Enchanted by the journey, for which we discern.

By moonlit rivers, in twilight's embrace,
We follow the roads to an enchanted place.
A world apart, in time and space,
Enchanted by the roads, we cherish the chase.

With spirits alight, on pathways divine,
We seek the wonders, on the roads that entwine.
A lifetime of adventures, on the thin line,
Enchanted by the roads less traveled, where we shine.

Journeys of the Restless Heart

Through tangled woods and shadowed paths,
Where light through gloom does part,
My weary soul in silence wraths,
On journeys of the restless heart.

With every step, a story grows,
Beneath the moon's soft glow,
The heart, a compass, surely knows,
Where winds of fate may blow.

Through trials and tears, the heart endures,
Its beat a steady drum,
In every ache, love reassures,
To the call of dreams, I succumb.

Past every peak and valley deep,
Where hidden treasures start,
My spirit vows a pledge to keep,
On journeys of the restless heart.

In quests for love, in realms unseen,
Where whispered fates impart,
I'll walk where few have ever been,
On journeys of the restless heart.

In Search of Unseen Lands

Beyond the maps where legends dwell,
And tales untold arise,
I set my sights on the unseen swell,
Under the vast, uncharted skies.

With curiosity as my guide,
Through tempests, calm, and gales,
I seek the places time forgot,
Where ancient whispers sail.

Amongst the stars, a path unfolds,
In the night's embrace, it stands,
A beacon for the bold and brave,
In search of unseen lands.

Each dawn reveals new mysteries,
Horizons broad and grand,
With every sunset's promise kept,
I tread through shifting sands.

So onwards in my quest I march,
With hope's light in my hands,
To find the beauty earth conceals,
In search of unseen lands.

Where Footprints Fade

Across the barren dunes of time,
My footsteps trace a lone design,
Yet winds whisper of a fateful chime,
Where footprints fade, but dreams align.

Underneath the ancient sky,
Where echoes speak and spirits sigh,
The past and future softly lie,
In lands where footprints fade and die.

Beyond the seas, beyond the glade,
Where nature's secrets are displayed,
My soul seeks refuge, unafraid,
Where footprints fade into the shade.

Through forgotten realms I roam,
Seeking what the earth has sown,
Learning that no matter where I'm blown,
Where footprints fade, I find my own.

In the quietude of twilight's embrace,
Where shadows dance and time erases,
Here, my weary heart retraces,
Where footprints fade in life's vast spaces.

Chasing the Sun's Retreat

Beneath the canvas of the waning light,
I chase the sun's retreat into the night,
A quest for warmth before the star's ignite,
In twilight hues, I find my solace bright.

Over hills aglow with fading fire,
Past rivers mirroring the sky's desire,
The sun's departure fuels my yearning higher,
As shadows lengthen, and the day expires.

Each step a race against the dimming glow,
I follow where the amber rivers flow,
Seeking secrets only sunsets know,
In the silent transition of day's bow.

With every dusk, I feel my spirit lift,
As if the sun's descent bestows a gift,
In colors splashed across the rift,
I find my heart in sun's eternal drift.

So when the stars their nightly vigil keep,
And the world in darkness seems to steep,
It's in the sun's last rays, so deep,
I lay my wishes, before I sleep.

Beyond the Horizon's Edge

Where the sky meets the sea, a whisper calls for me,
Beyond the horizon's edge, where dreams are free.
Sailing through the azure skies, with hope as my pledge,
In the realm of the endless, I walk the razor's edge.

Upon the canvas of the dawn, hues of freedom merge,
A journey beyond the known, on the thrill we surge.
Past the bounds of reality, where spirits allege,
To the realms untold, our paths diverge.

Stars gleam as beacons, in the night's silhouette,
Guiding through the darkness, on the course we set.
Beyond the horizon's edge, no regret, no fret,
Where our hearts yearn to be, in that eternal sunset.

With each step forward, the old world we shed,
New horizons beckon, by curiosity led.
Beyond the edge of tomorrow, where our spirits are fed,
In the land of the timeless, our souls are spread.

In the embrace of the horizon, where dreams align,
Past and future merge, in a dance divine.
Beyond the horizon's edge, where stars intertwine,
We find ourselves, in the infinite design.

Whispers of the Wayward Wind

In the silence of the night, whispers roam free,
Messages from the wayward wind, meant just for me.
Speaking in tongues of the ancient, under each tree,
Telling tales of old, setting my heart's questions free.

Through the rustling leaves, the wind converses,
In its embrace, the essence of time reverses.
Across the miles, the wayward wind traverses,
Carrying secrets, blessings, and curses.

It dances through the valleys, and over the hills,
Singing songs of the wild, that the heart fills.
A guide through the journey, it instills,
Wisdom of the Earth, in its chills and thrills.

With every gust, the wind whispers my name,
A call to journey beyond, a wild, untamed flame.
In the wayward wind's path, life's never the same,
It's a symphony of the world, a timeless acclaim.

So listen closely, to the whispers in the wind,
For it speaks of adventures, where dreams are pinned.
In its wayward journey, our souls are skinned,
To the core of our being, we're intimately twinned.

The Nomad's Compass

In my hand, the nomad's compass, pointing to the unknown,
Across deserts vast and mountains high, by the winds blown.
A guide to realms untouched, where the sun's never shone,
On the path of the wanderer, the seeds of curiosity sown.

Each direction calls with a promise, a story untold,
North to the icy realms, south to deserts bold.
East to the rising sun, west to sunsets gold,
The compass in my hand, my destiny it holds.

With the compass as my ally, through storms, I stride,
It leads me to the oasis, where dreams reside.
The nomad's path is lonesome, but wide,
With the compass by my side, I ride the tide.

Through forests deep and rivers wide, the compass leads,
To lands where the spirit of adventure feeds.
In the heart of the nomad, it plants the seeds,
Of quests and journeys, fulfilling unspoken needs.

So here I stand, with the compass in my grasp,
Ready to face the world, with a fervent clasp.
In the journey of a lifetime, my breath a gasp,
The nomad's compass, in my heart, I clasp.

Journeys Through Dreamscapes

In the realm of dreams, where time slows its pace,
I wander through landscapes, a serene space.
With each step, the echo of a forgotten embrace,
Journeys through dreamscapes, a terminal grace.

Visions of worlds, where the flowers sing,
Mountains whisper, and trees dance in a ring.
In the air, the scent of magic they bring,
Dreamscapes where imagination takes wing.

Under the moonlight, on a silvered lake,
Reflections of reality, in dreams, we remake.
Through the mists of sleep, our spirits wake,
In the fabric of dreams, our stories we stake.

Through the veils of slumber, a silent call,
In the garden of night, where shadows fall.
Journeys through dreamscapes, beyond the wall,
Where dreams and reality, in whispers, enthrall.

So close your eyes, and let your heart leap,
Into the realm of dreams, a vast, endless deep.
In the tapestry of the night, secrets to keep,
Journeys through dreamscapes, where thoughts seep.

Footfalls on the Bridge Between Worlds

In the shadowed vale where whispers dwell,
Above the chasm, wide and steep,
Footfalls echo, as if to tell
Of journeys made, in dreams, asleep.

On this bridge betwixt night and day,
Steps unsure, yet onward bound,
Travelers walk, fade, and fray,
In search of what cannot be found.

Here the fabric of realms does bend,
With each step, a story unfolds,
Footfalls on the bridge do wend,
Through mysteries that the cosmos holds.

Beneath a swath of starry skies,
Where two worlds in silence meet,
The bridge spans wide before our eyes,
With footfalls echoing, bittersweet.

In the heart of the endless between,
Where seconds stretch and hours blend,
There lies the path, seldom seen,
Where footfalls whisper, and worlds end.

Escape to the Land of the Eternal Sky

Beyond the grasp of time's tight fist,
Lies a realm where the ages roam,
A land of mist, by sunbeams kissed,
Calls the weary spirit home.

Over mountains crowned with snow,
Past the valleys, deep and wide,
Where the rivers of knowledge flow,
The Land of the Eternal Sky resides.

Eagles soar on breezes high,
Casting shadows on the ground below,
In a dance, with the endless sky,
They ride the winds where hopes might grow.

Here, the chains of fate unbind,
And heavy hearts can freely fly,
Within this realm, one may find,
A solace under the eternal sky.

In the embrace of the boundless blue,
Where dreams ascend and fears die,
Each soul may start life anew,
And find peace in the Eternal Sky.

Trailing the Scent of Distant Rains

Upon the breeze, a whisper soft,
Carries the scent of rain to come,
From dusty earth to canopy aloft,
It calls, to the parched, it hums.

Through leaves and across the plains,
It travels, a harbinger lush and sweet,
A promise of life, in gentle rains,
In its scent, distant storms meet.

With each droplet that from clouds fall,
The earth rejoices, the rivers sing,
The scent of rain, like a lover's call,
Brings hope on its dampened wing.

This trail we follow, through storm and calm,
Led by the fragrance that precedes the storm,
In the scent of rain, a soothing balm,
That heals the world, and allows it to transform.

The distant rains, when they finally arrive,
Quench the earth, the soul, the air,
In their scent, the world comes alive,
A reminder, that life is beyond compare.

Unraveling the Threads of Destiny

In the loom of fate, threads intertwine,
Each life a pattern, unique and vast,
In every strand, a story-line,
From the first breath to the last.

Destiny's weave, tight and complex,
Holds us in its inexorable grip,
Yet in our hands, the future flex,
As off the loom's edge, threads may slip.

With each choice made, a thread is pulled,
Altering patterns, weaving anew,
In the tapestry of time, rich and full,
Our hands can change the view.

The threads of destiny, so intricately spun,
In every moment, they unwind,
Under the gaze of the setting sun,
New paths, by our own hands, designed.

So with each day, let us weave with care,
Our destinies, in colors bright and bold,
For in our stories, everyone shares,
A part of the tapestry, unique and untold.

www.ingramcontent.com/pod-product-compliance
Lightning Source LLC
LaVergne TN
LVHW020422070526
838199LV00003B/232